The Book of Allah

A Play on
The Conflict between Light and Darkness

To watch the play, please scan the following QR Code:
The Book of Allah
A Play on
The Conflict between Light and Darkness

Dr. Sultan bin Muhammad Al-Qasimi

The Book of Allah

A Play on
The Conflict between Light and Darkness

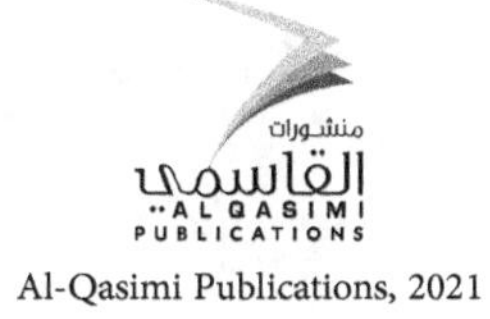

Al-Qasimi Publications, 2021

The Book of Allah
A Play on The Conflict between Light and Darkness
First published in 2018 in Arabic as "Kitab Allah – Al-Siraa' bayna Al-Nur wa
Al-Zalam" by : Al-Qasimi Publications
Author: Dr. Sultan bin Muhammad Al-Qasimi (United Arab Emirates)
Publisher Name: Al-Qasimi Publications
Sharjah, United Arab Emirates
Edition: First
Year of publication: 2021
© All rights reserved:
Al-Qasimi publications
Sharjah, United Arab Emirates

Translated from the Arabic by: Dr. Ahmed Ali

ISBN: 978-9948-469-49-0
Printing Permission: National Media Council, Abu Dhabi, UAE
No. MC 01-03-8798988, Date: 05-08-2021

Age Classification: E
The age group that matches the content of the books was classified according
to the age classification issued by the National Council for Media

----

Al- Qasimi Publications, Al Tarfa, Sheikh Mohammed Bin Zayed Road
PO Box 64009 Sharjah, United Arab Emirates
Tel: 0097165090000, Fax: 0097165520070
Email: info@aqp.ae

CONTENTS

Cast of Characters

- The Nūrānis (Followers of Light), dressed in white garments and turbans

- Commander of Light

- A man's voice (A Caller)

- First man

- Second man

- Third man

- A group of scholars

- Eastern delegates

- Commander of the Eastern delegates

- Western delegates (dressed in Western clothes)

- Commander of the Western delegates

- The Żalāmis (The Followers of Darkness)

- Commander of Darkness

- A group of women

- Two men

- A group of men (with spotlights)

Place:

A huge hall

Time:

The present

Scene One

Place:

A huge wide hall, unidentified.

Time:

The present

The scene opens to a huge hall with the lights on. A rectangular table is in the centre. Hanging from the ceiling above the table is a copy of the Holy Qur'an. It is tilted at a 45° angle towards the audience. Strong spotlights from all direction are focused on it. On the walls are stacked books with reed pens and inkpots.

A group of men (the Nūrānis) in white garments and turbans enter the hall. They are humming some Qur'anic verses, and are led by the Commander of Light. They come to the stage one by one, from the right and left; each holding an open copy of the Qur'an from which he reads. They walk round the table. When they are all there, they take their seats round the table. They place their Qur'an copies in front of them. At the top of the table, their Commander sits.

A voice is heard saying:

"The Messenger of Allah, Peace Be Upon Him, said:

O, people, I leave amongst you (two things), if you hold on tightly to them, you will never go astray: the Book of Allah and the Sunnah of His Prophet."

The group members at the table disperse in the hall and head for the walls. Each one takes a book, a notebook, and an inkpot, then returns to sit at the table to read and make notes.

Their voices echo in unison:

With the Message from on High

And the teachings of Islam,

We spread prosperity and peace;

With knowledge and faith,

We protect our homelands.

Blackout

Scene Two

The same hall as in Scene One. The same lights, stacked books, and the Qur'an copy suspended from the ceiling.

The voices of the group are still echoing:

With the Message from on High

And the teachings of Islam,

We spread prosperity and peace;

With knowledge and faith,

We protect our homelands.

A man enters the hall pushing a mobile table on wheels. There are chemicals and tools on top of it. He conducts some interesting experiments, and says:

I am Jābir ibn Ḥayyān al-Azdī. I lived in the great city of Kufa between 103 AH and 199 AH (722 – 815 CE). I am known as the Father of Chemistry. My research has led to major advances in chemical sciences. I also invented the first distillation device in the world.

The group is heard chanting:

With the Message from on High

And the teachings of Islam,

We spread prosperity and peace;

With knowledge and faith,

We protect our homelands.

Another man walks into the hall pushing a table with various equipment, a musical instrument (Oud/lute) and an ostrich feather plectrum. The man says:

"I am Ya'coub ibn Ishaq al-Kindi. I lived between 185 AH and 260 AH (805 – 873 CE). I am a scholar of mathematics, physics, astronomy, philosophy, medicine, engineering, pharmacology, chemistry and geography. There is also another discipline you may not know that I am well-versed in, that is, music. I am the first person to document the notes of the Arabic musical scale and set its principles. Let me play some tunes for you."

He takes the Oud and plectrum, then masterfully starts to play some music and sing.

The group is heard chanting:

With the Message from on High

And the teachings of Islam,

We spread prosperity and peace;

With knowledge and faith,

We protect our homelands.

A third man walks in. In his hands are some devices used for measuring the distance between planetary objects. He says:

"I am al-Hassan ibn al-Haytham. I lived between 353 AH and 431 AH (965 CE – 1040 CE). I am a polymath specialized in optics, astronomy, engineering, ophthalmology, and optical recognition. My discoveries have led to major changes to the optical concepts that were dominant at the time. I established the science of light. Scientists before me believed that when light from the eyes falls on an object, we are able to see it. "Why doesn't the light come out of the eyes in the dark?", I asked. I then introduced my theory and proved that light reflects from an object and then passes to one's eyes; that's how we see".

The group is heard chanting:

With the Message from on High

And the teachings of Islam,

We spread prosperity and peace;

With knowledge and faith,

We protect our homelands.

The chanting continues after the names of other scientists are called out.

Voice:

Muhammad al-Khawārizmī

Abu Bakr al-Rāzī

Abu Nasr al-Farābī

Abu al-Rayhān al-Birūnī.

Scene Three

The hall, as in Scene Two.

The Commander of Light is sitting at the table in his white garment. A group of people enter from the right side of the stage. They are coming from the East and dressed in colourful garments. The Commander of the Eastern Delegates greets the Commander of Light saying:

Peace be with you, Commander of Light.

A voice answering the greeting is heard.

The Eastern Delegates chant:

From the far Orient, we have come

Offering allegiance and love,

And seeking the eternal wisdom

Of the message from on High above.

*The chanting is accompanied by artistic formations
using colourful fabrics.*

**Afterwards, another group walks on to the stage
from the left coming from the West and dressed in
Western attires. The Commander of the Western
Delegates greets the Commander of Light, saying:**

Peace be with you, Commander of Light.

A voice answering the greeting is heard.

The Eastern Delegates chant:

In the West we lived in utter darkness,

Ignorance and decadence reigned supreme;

Today, we've come to learn and witness

How to fulfill a long-lost dream.

The chanting is accompanied by western dancing.

**Then, the two delegates join in dancing while they
all sing together:**

O, Fort of Islam, where all nations meet,

Spread your wings of knowledge o'er us;

Oasis of prosperity, safety and peace,

Teach us your Faith, your Arts and Science.

Blackout

Scene Four

The same hall as in the previous scene.
The men at the table are extending their arms on it, resting their heads and sleeping. The spotlights on the Qur'an copy are off.

A voice is heard reciting a verse from the Qur'an:

All, the Almighty says: "And so they were succeeded by a posterity who completely neglected their salah (daily prayers) and followed their lusts. Consequently, they will meet evil."

Into the hall comes a group of Żalāmis** (Followers of the Darkness), **dressed in black unitards that leave only their eyes uncovered. in all directions they jump and cackle like crows. They jump on the table and climb on top of one another to reach the Qur'an

copy hanging from the ceiling. The one at the top snatches it and shouts:

"O, Commander of Darkness, here is the book of Allah. Take it and judge with it."

The Commander of Darkness takes the copy and says:

"First, throw these imposters who claim to be Muslim, out of here."

Each Żalāmi pulls a Nūrāni out of the hall. Then, they return and sit at the table where the Commander of Darkness is sitting at the top. They ask him:

'O, Commander of Darkness, what is your decision about the captives we have?'

The Commander of Darkness:

"Behead them with a Cleaver."

Some of them leave, and then return, each driving in front of them a prisoner and grabbing them by the hair. They start the beheading while joyously screaming.

One of them asks:

"O, Commander of Darkness, what do we do with the female captives?

Commander of Darkness:

Bring them in.

A group of women dressed in black are brought in.

Commander of Darkness (to his men):

Each one of you takes one of them.

Each Żalāmi grabs one of the women who scream loudly.

The Żalāmis are heard barking like dogs as they chase the women:

Woof, woof!

They all mix as the chase and screams continue:

Woof, woof!

Commander of Darkness:

Who would like to have better and more beautiful women than these?
Four houris in Paradise.
Yes, four houris in Paradise.

Let those who would like this come forward and blow themselves up. You will then die as a martyr and will be taken straight to Paradise where the houris are.

The loud sounds of explosions are heard and the flames become visible.

The Żalāmis chant:

The Qur'an is ours!

The Faith is ours!

The Sharia is ours!

The rule is ours!

Blackout

Scene Five

The setting is the same as in the scenes before. The stage is in darkness.

The Żalāmis in their black garments are busy round the table.

Enter two men in white attire. They stand at one side of the stage chatting.

The first man:

We cannot destroy them with canons and guns.

The other man:

So, how can we destroy them?

The first man:

With the spread of light. This is the only way.

The other man:

But how?

The first man:

We have to bring the light into all aspects of our life.

The other man:

Let us act immediately.

A group of men dressed in white enter the stage; on their heads are spotlights and they chant:

O, Allah, place light in my heart,

light in my tongue,

light in my hearing,

light in my sight,

light behind me,

light in front of me,

light above me,

light below me;

O, Allah, give me Light.

The Żalamis are disturbed by the chants and the lights.

The stage is fully lit.

The Żalāmis try to escape while the Nūrānis chase

them to retrieve the copy of the Qur'an from them. The Qur'an copy changes hands and it eventually ends in the hands of the Commander of Light, who raises it high. The Żalāmis start falling to the ground one after the other.

Pointing at the dead bodies of the Żalāmis, the Commander of Light says:

Drive these debased people out of here.

The Nūrānis start pulling the corpses out of the stage while chanting:

Allah is great, really and truly;

Praise be to Allah abundantly;

Day and night to Allah be glory;

There is no god but Allah, the one and only.

To His servant He granted victory,

Raised in honour the status of His soldiers,

And Alone He defeated the confederates;

There is no god but Allah.

Qur'an recitation is heard.

Voice:

Allah, glorified be He, says:

And say, Truth has come and falsehood has

vanished away. Behold! falsehood is ever bound to vanish. And We are gradually revealing of the Qur'an *(that teaching)* which is *(the cause of)* healing and mercy for the believers. But this (revelation) only leads the unjust persons from loss to loss.

In the meantime, the copy of the Qur'an is restored to its original place, high up on the stage suspended from the ceiling.

The group repeats:

And say, Truth has come and falsehood has vanished away. Behold! falsehood is ever bound to vanish.

A voice is heard shouting:

The women have arrived; let them join in our celebrations. Make room for them.

The women walk onto the stage, dressed in white garments and white veils whose edges they hold in their hands spreading them like the wings of butterflies.

The books are restored on the shelves.

All join in chanting:

With the Message from on High

And the teachings of Islam,

We spread prosperity and peace;

With knowledge and faith,

We protect our homelands.

The End

9 789948 469490